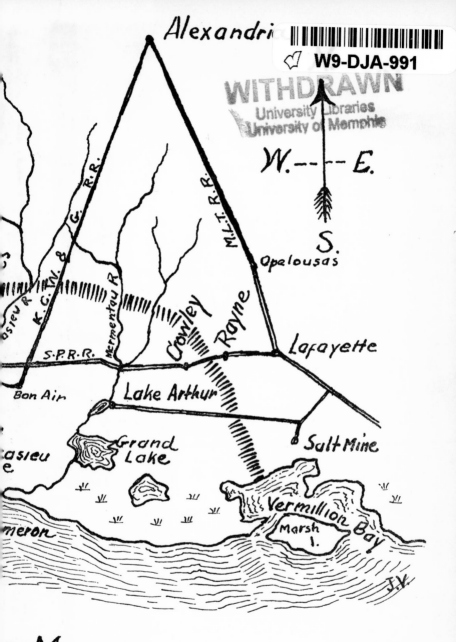

Mexico

rles Daily Press, 1895 Ed.)
part.)

STREAK O' LEAN

AND

A STREAK O' FAT

With trembling hand
I autograph this to a journalist,
with best wishes though my
old friend The Virgolas —

Jos. Vincent
July 25, 1964
Brit. Tex —

Streak O' Lean
and
a
Streak O' Fat

By

JOSEPH J. VINCENT

With illustrations by the author

VANTAGE PRESS

NEW YORK   WASHINGTON   HOLLYWOOD

PREFACE

THE PURPOSE of this little book is fourfold.

First, the writer wishes to make a record of the way the Gulf Coast pioneers of Southwest Louisiana and Southeast Texas struggled to live and to gain a foothold in the flat country, midst floods, droughts, pests and disease, to form the foundation for the now wealthy empire of oil, timber, cattle, rice, fish, and fur, lying approximately between the Mermentau River in Louisiana and the Trinity River in Texas.

Second, I wish to extol the merits of those pioneer men and women whose ingenuity, fortitude, and diligence equaled the spirit of our more publicized Pilgrims, Puritans, or western frontiersmen.

Third, I would show thousands of natives of the Gulf Coast that their own forefathers were as hardy a people and their traditions, prestige, etc., just as illustrious as those of any who so proudly point to their Mayflower ancestors.

Fourth, I would show our present generation that boys and girls HAVE married, raised and educated families, and even grown to wealth, without FHA, PWA, CCC, social security, subsidies, old-age pensions, and similar Government patronage, and that people have actually "started from the bottom and WORKED to the top," that truly, "Where there is a will, there is a way," and that "Necessity is the Mother of Invention"; one should not quit or be discouraged if one fails to get that scholarship, loan, or job. In short, a fourth purpose of this book is to glorify a time when security depended on the individual and not on the Government.

The only Government help extended in those early times was the opportunity to the settler to obtain a grant of 160 acres of land for a homestead, an opportunity with its counterpart today in the free educational facilities, free libraries, and free highways afforded every citizen.

NOTE: Let it be said here and now that it is not the intent of the author to recommend that we go back to old standards, but rather to assure those who do not realize it that they have a large storehouse of physical and mental resources from which they may draw when the going gets rough. IT CAN BE DONE! IT HAS BEEN DONE!

Joseph J. Vincent

Acknowledgments

I HAD the honor of showing my sketches of early homesteads, which I had drawn as a hobby, to the Beaumont, Texas, chapter of the Daughters of the Republic of Texas, April 3, 1952. After the showing and a lecture, Mrs. J. A. Raney, Mrs. J. H. Winton, Mrs. Claudia Norvell, Mrs. T. S. Reed, Mrs. Howard Gardner, Mrs. Maude Richardson and other members seemed very enthusiastic and urged that the material be published. Thus was STREAK O' LEAN AND A STREAK O' FAT born.

Dr. and Mrs. John E. Gray, Mrs. A. Stuart Hurst, Mr. Caldwell McFaddin, Mr. Willie Gilbert, Mr. Willie Hebert, Mr. Walter Casey, and Mr. and Mrs. J. E. Broussard gave useful criticisms and encouragement.

"Old Timer," history contributor of the Beaumont Journal, helped with factual material. Mr. Ted Farnes of the same paper helped in many ways. Miss Evie Payne, of the South Park High School Library, helped with reference material.

Miss Beatrice Burnaby typed the manuscript and helped with the mechanics of the little book.

Mr. and Mrs. Joe Doré and Joe Vincent of Crowley, Louisiana, read the manuscript and gave valuable help on the pictures on rice and cattle. Benson Vincent of Hackberry, Louisiana, and Sam Vincent of Sulphur, Louisiana, gave assistance on the cow brands of Louisiana.

Last, but certainly not least, was the help of my wife, Mrs. Esther Vincent, who not only helped and encouraged with the production of STREAK O' LEAN AND A STREAK O' FAT, but allowed her home to be messed up for months during which time the many sketches were being made.

To all of the above I am truly grateful.

J. J. V.

WHENCE THE NAME

THE WRITER received many inquiries about the title *Streak O' Lean and a Streak O' Fat* when the first edition was being sold. These came, of course, from other than southern states, and certainly none from Arkansas, where the University football team is called "The Razorbacks." And a good name it is, too, for the razorback is tough, fearsome, and vicious. Using his sharp tusks as weapons, he has slit many a dog to shreds.

Before the days of registered breeds, almost all homesteaders had a few of these semiwild hogs which, because of their narrow and lean backs, were called razorbacks. They roamed the woods and swamps, feeding on acorns, roots, and nut grass, requiring neither care nor fencing. They figured in the economy of southern settlers when, after the fall frost, it was "hog-killing time."

The bacon from these itinerants, if tough, was not unsavory. According to the homesteaders, it was streaked with lean and fat, depending on the abundance or scarcity of wild forage.

Hence the name means good days and bad days, or lean times and fat times.

TABLE OF CONTENTS

INTRODUCTION

Sam's Marsh   oyster bayou   Twin oaks   gator Cove

The cow hands, hunters, trappers and others who had to find their way about the marsh country in the early days of unmarked trails, were often guided by crude diagrams drawn in the sands of the little alkali flats along the edge of the marshes; the crude pen drawings in this little book are for the same purpose; they are not intended to be art. High points of observation place horizons out of position, but allow better details of tools with which the people worked—

J.J.V.

Bill's House

J.V.

13

PIONEERS

FRONTIERS—like little boys—are not fixed. Wherever and whenever a plowpoint tears its way into new land, or an axe chops its way through virgin forests, or a thought penetrates past accepted superstitions, a frontier is born and men become pioneers.

Civilization's progress depends on frontiers. They are successful or not, depending upon the energy, intrepidity, resourcefulness, stamina, and spirituality of the frontiersmen. Jamestown, Virginia, had almost failed because of lack of energy, but wise old Captain John Smith issued the famous edict, "He who does not work shall not eat," and the outpost survived. The Columbus venture would have failed had the less intrepid sailors had their way. The success of the Antarctic frontier would most certainly have fallen short had not Commander Byrd resourcefully devised means by which to hold at bay dementing loneliness. And many a frontier has pushed onward that would have been lost in oblivion but for a turning to the acknowledgment of the power and presence of God.

If a frontier is established, takes root, and disappears as a rude pattern of life to become blended with a nurtured identity, we regard the frontier as having been successful. It has evolved into something with which to be reckoned. Thus some frontiers appear to be successful which actually carry civilization backward. Al Capone, in the 1920's, was apparently successful in pioneering organized crime on a scale never before ventured. This frontier, succeeding to high places, challenging the frontiers of organized society, still survives. Herod pioneered in martyrizing Christians—another frontier which seems to endure in the

15

form of the greatest of aggressive threats to the idea of Christ-likeness.

Boundary lines grow more important rather than less so, with each advance toward civilization's ultimate total recognition of the rights of individual entities. It is with this profound respect for the significance of every frontier in the infinite scheme of things that this treatment of a frontier in the inland central Gulf Coast section has been prepared.

The founders of this central Gulf Coast frontier are not too long gone. Some of them are living today, their pioneer trails marked by a lively wake. The afterglow of the driving spirit which inspired their conquests more than half a century ago is mirrored in the virile calibre of their descendants.

Some of the family names which figure in this recent frontier and which are found lengthily in present-day rosters of the area, are Boudreaux, Broussard, LeBlanc, LeBlue, LeDeux, Vincent, and others. Such names suggest migration from the older, more settled areas around New Orleans. Other family names then and now prominent include Fox, Gonzales, O'Lera, McFaddin, Perkins, and West, settlers who came largely from the West and South, bringing in some instances their negro ex-slaves. Then Chalkley, Drew, Gradwold, Kahn, Kaufman, Kraus, Levy, Miller, and other families came largely from the North, to build sawmills and to set up stores, which later became the nuclei of towns like Lake Charles, Louisiana, and Beaumont and Orange, Texas.

With the influx of "Yankees" about 1900, lured by tales of rice riches, came mules and modern farm machinery, and the building of rice canals. The Findleys, Ducons, Weights, Spaldings, Fosters, and others, were names which pillared the growth of towns like Crowley, Jennings, and Iowa, Louisiana.

The earliest comers to the Gulf Coast country settled along the banks of rivers and bayous, partly because they had come down the Mississippi in boats or on rafts, and partly because water meant communication with the outside world. Much, therefore, of the land along the pleasant rivers and sleepy bayous

16

had already been homesteaded by the beginning of the Twentieth Century. Thus it was that the children of these earlier settlers must push farther inland for new home sites.

Young people who had married and were seeking new homes usually put a few possessions in a small wagon and drove to a piece of vacant land which had by some means been previously selected.

The pen-and-ink sketches which follow will help to recreate some of the "feel" of frontier life. And whether or not one recognizes it, the qualities required to establish that—or any—frontier, are as vital today, for less visible, less tangible frontiers that demand individual manifestations of vision, fortitude, and zeal from every living being.

It is not with awe so much as with exultation, not so much with pity as with pride that the example of these immediate forbears of our present heritage is intimated.

As you turn them, dear reader, may these pages, like successive mirrors, image back to you the qualities within yourself that make you, too, on frontiers not yet formed, an immortal pioneer!

WHERE ARE YOU FOLKS GOING?

WHEN the pioneers began pushing into the interior from the river and bayou banks which had already been settled by earlier home seekers, the most common means of transportation was the flat bottom boat by water and the ox cart by land.

The illustration here shows two families moving out into the new country, one by land, the other by water, each with a common interest, a home.

These two families will both endeavor to find a place for their homes as near a stream and woods as possible.

One can easily imagine the friendly greeting and question, WHERE ARE YOU FOLKS GOING?

THE BEGINNING OF THE BEGINNING

THE PICTURE on the opposite page is a representation of how, with meager tools and abundant vision and industry, the early settlers in the inland central Gulf Coast country began wresting from the earth's elements the foundations of a new life.

The little wagon in which they have arrived, and which may have served as a shelter until the house was built, contained perhaps two or three coils of barbed wire, a homemade harrow, a plow, spade, rake, hoe, axe, and other simple possessions. In some cases, it also included the lumber they would use in building the first makeshift shelter. If there were no nearby woods, many a trip will have been made in the wagon to haul the lumber with which the little house is finally built, set on cypress blocks if available.

As soon as possible, when the house is near completion, the homesteader plows a garden spot, using the same faithful horses which pulled the wagon to the site, and while his wife works the soil and plants the seed, the head of this pioneer family will string around the garden plot a fence, for there will be chickens and prairie "varmints" from which it must be protected.

With his shotgun and dog, he hunts for the meat which the family uses for the first few months.

As a wedding or leavetaking present to them on their departure from their previous home, a pig had perhaps been given to the homesteaders, and a little pen for it has been built near or even adjacent to the house, so as to fatten it up for fall butchering.

Many great plantations and ranches started from just such simple beginnings as suggested by this sketch.

21

Taking Root

AFTER a few months, interesting developments begin to take form in this humble homestead.

Trees had to be planted; the wagon has been used to haul saplings of shade and fruit trees which have been planted with much thought as to where they will be needed for shade and protection. They are now showing signs of taking root.

The garden has by this time usually begun bearing in this virgin soil, and is now yielding beans, corn, cucumbers, turnips, and other easily raised vegetables.

The water is being obtained from a well which, by this time, has been dug, and which, as soon as their prosperity will permit, will be equipped by the homesteader with a wheel and a rope by which the lifting of the buckets is made easier.

The chicken house which has been built has become essential because of the marauding opossums, mink, coons, and occasional foxes.

In one of the infrequent trips to town (perhaps 15 miles away) a zinc tub has been purchased. It now hangs on the side of the house, awaiting the occasions for which it is taken down —the Saturday night bath or weekly wash.

SETTLING THE LOWLANDS

SOME of these settlers were so fortunate as to find vacant lands in that part of the country where the cypress trees grow, where there were marshes with abundant game. In such cases, the pattern for the homesteader was a little different from that previously described.

Hard, continuous, painstaking work was the order of those days, and everyone in the family participated. While the head of the family is butchering the hog, which he has just scalded in the barrel at the right (the water having been heated in the washpot in the foreground), his wife is pounding rice in the homemade wooden mortar to remove the hulls from the rice grain.

From the cypress logs, boards were split with which he covered his house, and often from these easily worked cypress logs the homesteader made all the lumber out of which the house was built. Some of these old cypress houses are still standing and function as the kitchen of some large plantation home which, years later, was added to the original structure.

The simple tools used by the pioneer in preparing his lumber were a froe and mallet. The froe was driven into the log cuts with a wooden mallet. In this way the short boards were split off in somewhat even thicknesses in conformity with the regular cypress grain. These were cached in the little rack or "horse" which can be seen in the sketch, and the operator used his drawing knife to shave the board down to the desired thickness.

Some of these cypress-shingled roofs are known to have lasted forty years.

The rice was grown in the little "Providence patch" in the rear of the house. Somewhere near is a corn patch, mutely testified to by the corn-grinder nailed to the smokehouse.

The frozen foods locker of pioneer days was the smoke-house, from the roof of which hangs a brace of wild duck which the homesteader has killed during the early morning hours. Several slabs of bacon and sausage hang from poles in this little house, cured by the smoke from the hardwood fires. The remainder of the hog was salted down or covered with melted lard in a wooden barrel.

The mud chimney was the architectural and engineering masterpiece of the homesteader's efforts and his neighbors' assistance. It was a community project, and the little weed seen atop the chimney was a significant feature. This little sprig served not only to crown the completion of an important feature of the home but was a quaint souvenir of his neighbors' kindness. It was said of this bit of bulrush that by the time it rotted, the homesteaders would be well enough started to hold a dance, which in Louisiana was known as a "fais-do-do."

The barrel at the corner of the house is an ash barrel into which rainwater is allowed to drip for the purpose of making the "box" lye which was used by the wife in making her soap. Here again, the old washpot plays an important role. In it the fats which the newly butchered hog provided were boiled, water added, and then the lye, to make the unperfumed and effectual soap for personal and laundering use.

The fringe of cypress trees in the background is the home-steader's firewood and lumber yard; but it is more than that: it is also his source of mattress filling. On the barbed wire fence hangs moss which has been gathered from the trees. It is drying, and after the weathering has sloughed off the soft outer tissues, the almost wirelike inner fibre will be stuffed into a hand-sewn ticking for the homesteader's new mattress.

THE HARD PRAIRIE

NOT ALL homesteaders were lucky enough to get near a stream of water. Some pushed out into the bald prairies, where later, with the aid of barbed wire and the windmill, the beginnings of what proved to be a great cattle ranch took root.

This little home is a typical prairie homestead, where a few trees have been planted, a shed serves for a barn, and a herd is in its beginning stages. And, of course, there are the ever-present dog and cat.

The fine prairie grass made it unnecessary to feed the cattle, hence the reason for such beginnings of cattle ranches.

Under the shed, which was later expanded, he usually kept his tools and used it to build many of his work tools, such as a harrow and drag. The shed also served to provide shade, since there were no trees.

The struggle for existence in this environment was indeed a hard one.

The Scrub Oak Country

This little homestead seems a little friendlier because it has been established long enough to have a garden, chickens, a well, and a few trees. The man of the house has made a work bench back by the chimney, and a permanent outhouse has been built. The cat and dog, and the mother and her little child, seem to be having fun in front of the house. The indispensable woodpile and washpot are in evidence.

This homestead is located, as you can see, not too far from the scrub oak knolls and flats. However, what appears to be scrub oak could be Cherokee thorn bushes, the remnants of a day when the prairie people attempted to keep their cattle separated by thorn bushes, before the advent of barbed wire.

Come Inside, Please

Here, just for fun, we look into one end of the homesteader's house. You notice that the house has no ceiling and that the furnishings are the simplest, although not without certain friendly aspects. Note the little wash shelf, which holds up a wash pan and the proverbial red cedar bucket containing water for washing and drinking. You will notice the common drinking cup or gourd hanging above the wash pan, and the family towel on a nail nearby.

At the table is a "store bought" chair, while all the rest of the furniture is homemade.

The wood box behind the stove was an institution in the homesteader's dwelling. Many a little child has sat on this wood box while he talked to his mother about the little things which interested him. Then, too, filling this wood box was often the responsibility of this same child. Truly, the wood box was a large factor in the lives of country boys and girls.

Notice the preserved fruits on the shelves, and the dish towel drying behind the stove, the kerosene lamp, and the coffee mill.

I wonder what is in the trunk? A good guess would be that it contains a dress or two, sheets, and pillow cases, and a few little things which the mother had given to the daughter when, as a bride, she left home.

This Way, Please

Here we have the other end of the house, with the bedstead built in the corner, the mosquito bar (there were no screens then), and the piece quilt. There is one rocking chair, perhaps brought from home, a Bible on the shelf under the mirror, a gun in the corner, and a kerosene lamp on the mantle. There may even be a sheepskin by the side of the bed.

Sometimes pumpkins, melons, or fruit were stored under the bed, at least until baby arrived and a "trundle" bed filled the space.

WELL ON THE WAY

WE ARE well on our way, apparently. Four or five years have passed. The trees have grown quite a bit, and the barn has been enlarged. The little garden has been expanded into a fairly large field.

The homesteader has accumulated a few head of cattle. Behind the barn is a "lot," the name given to the small pen where the horses were kept at night, or it may have been a cow pen, which the next year would become a turnip patch.

The picture indicates that here a couple of good American citizens and their children have, through diligence, firmly rooted themselves. This is as truly the foundation of America as its counterpart in the North, East, or West, and these people are as great as the pioneers of any other section.

Fringe Country Homestead

We have here the more fortunate of the homesteaders. We shall call them the homesteaders of the fringe country, because they live along that line which parallels the Gulf Coast, where the pine trees come down from the North to meet the cypress trees coming up from the South.

Probably these people had a little easier time than the homesteaders in the prairie country or in the piney woods sections. Here, you will notice, a rail fence made from hardwood and a pieux fence made from the friendly cypress trees. Notice the two men using a windlass to roll out a cypress log. In the foreground, you will notice the tools with which they will make posts, boards, and fence material out of the cypress log.

Of course, where there are cypress trees, there are streams, which usually mean fish. In the piney and hardwoods country, there were turkeys, squirrel, and deer, and in marsh country, there were ducks and geese.

A pirogue is in the foreground. The people in the bayou country were very skillful in the handling of this little boat.

In the lower left corner, you will notice three mullen plants. The pioneers made syrup from leaves, which they gave children for croup and colds.

Homestead de Luxe

This represents the "last word" in homesteading. Probably no homestead was ever as complete as the one pictured here. The purpose of the sketch is only to show to what extent the homestead might have been developed during one generation.

A family so established lived in relative luxury. The writer remembers that the "store bill" for one year for a similar homestead was a total of $61, which included mainly coffee, sugar, flour, and hardware purchases, such as nails and staples. All the other essentials were produced from the land.

You will notice here that there is much activity in connection with the syrup making, which was a sort of social event in those days. Syrup making time was looked forward to in communities because everyone had a lot of fun. A few of the neighbors have gathered to help. The young boys are playing in the bagasse pile which is a slight distance from the cane mill. Bagasse was the cane stalks after the juices had been squeezed out.

An interesting item is the banking of the cane tops (center left). In this way, the homesteader saved cane seed for the next year's planting.

You will notice chickens, ducks, geese, guineas, turkeys, and sheep. Probably no homestead would have had all of these. The hog in the pen, the milk cow out at the barn, and the garden, with the other animals and fowls, assured the homesteaders of abundant food.

Probably the reason these people are so prosperous is because they live in the fringe country, as can be seen by the hardwood and pine trees in the background.

SMOKESCREEN

REMEMBER, this is before the day of screens. For many years, houses were not screened. But there were certainly as many mosquitoes then as now.

This picture shows a homestead in the rather early stages. It is perhaps near the end of the day, with the father and mother of the family sitting on the front porch. The mosquitoes are getting bad as darkness approaches. The children have been sent out to the windward side of the house to build a "smoke."

They first start a fire, and then cover it with bitterweeds and dry cow manure. The resulting smoke was unpleasant to the mosquitoes and kept them away for so long as the smoke lasted. (But I have often wondered which was worse—the smoke or the mosquitoes!)

OCCASION FOR HASTE

THE BIG drug companies of America have, from time to time, published pictures of the country doctor, and many calendars have as their subject, the stork carrying a baby across the skies.

The country doctor, as he should have been, has been glorified for his perilous trips in pioneer country to bring children into the world. However, doctors were not always available, and here we have the father of this pioneer family applying the whip to his faithful steed, with the hope of reaching home with "Aunt Annie" before the baby arrives. Many people now living were brought into the world by these faithful women. But actually much tragedy lurked in their trails. Many mothers, though hardy, died during or after childbirth because of improper care and unsanitary methods.

One can hardly estimate the fortitude which our grandmothers must have had when they set off in the wagon which was to carry them to remote locations when they knew that eventually they would have to bear children under such circumstances. Truly this courage of pioneer women to carry their roles into motherhood was one of the important foundation stones of the civilization they were helping to build.

Wash Day

Do you know what a "battler" is? The woman in the picture is using one. After dipping the clothes in the water of the gully and soaping them with homemade soap, she "battled," or beat, the clothes with this paddlelike device.

For the children, washday was sometimes a lot of fun! The little girl is crayfishing, and the little boy is sailing his boat. Sometimes the little boy and his little sister got a switching before the end of the day, for falling into the gully or for throwing mud.

Washing clothes down at the gully was usually the privilege of the people in the fringe country, because the little gullies fed the larger streams, along the banks of which the cypress, pine, and hardwood trees grew. In the higher country, the washing was done around the house, the clothes being washed in tubs after being boiled in the washpot, the water for both being hauled out of a surface well.

The Always Welcome Overnight Guest

"Hello! May I stay all night?"

This call at the front gate brings a rush of dogs, whining, snarling, and barking, and for a few minutes the homesteader inside cannot understand the words of his visitor because of the uproar, but he already knows the story: the traveler wishes to spend the night.

After the dogs are quieted down, the traveler is welcomed, invited to unsaddle his horse and to take him around to the barn for feed and water, and then is ushered into the little house, where he is given every hospitality.

Usually on such occasions the whole family would sit up later than usual, listening to the tales of the traveler. It was in this way that they heard much of the news of the day, and the traveler was usually a welcome guest.

After breakfast the next morning, the traveler usually offers to pay his host, but this is seldom accepted. Upon departing, the traveler is given instructions as to the road ahead, and just before he sets off, the housewife may give him some food which he stores in his saddle bag for the journey.

Going to the Dance

DID YOUR grandmother ever tell you about a side saddle?

The horse in the picture is entering the water, and the young lady seated on his back (who might be your great-grandmother) is riding side saddle. Gentlewomen always rode side saddle then, and in 1952 a great national magazine had, as its cover, a picture of the beautiful young Queen of England, gracefully riding her English side saddle before her thousands of subjects.

Side saddles in this country were before the day of the automobile and before roads were good enough even for horse and buggy traffic.

But boys will be boys and girls will be girls, and here are some young people going to a dance. It will probably start early Saturday evening and last until the wee hours of Sunday morning.

The orchestra at these dances was usually composed of one or two of the oldtime fiddlers, and in the French country of Louisiana, an accordion. The Louisiana French people called the dance a "fais-de-deaux."

Sometimes these were benefit dances, where the guests could buy food. In Louisiana particularly, it was usually gumbo, and the proceeds were turned over to the local church.

47

Time to Think

It is said that no great building, factory, or monument ever existed that did not first exist in the mind of its creator. One of the great advantages country boys and girls had was that they had time to think, to draw mind pictures.

A good time for thinking, for a country boy, was during his walks through the woods or while on errands to the neighbor's house. Let's call this little boy Joe. It is Saturday afternoon. A hog has been butchered at Joe's house and his father has said to him, "Joe, jump on the horse and take some of this fresh meat over to the neighbors." (There were no deep freezes then, and fresh meat was usually shared with neighbors not living too far away.)

So Joe climbs upon his horse and starts through the woods over the prairie, or across little streams, toward a neighbor's house. His legs are very likely too short to reach his father's stirrups, but the horse is gentle, and Joe knows how to ride. So generally there is nothing to disturb his thinking.

However, once in a while a rabbit or squirrel runs across the trail in front of the horse, frightening him, and he dodges out from under Joe. On some occasions, the horse was so frightened that he ran off and left Joe to walk home.

Such vicissitudes did not alarm Joe, however, and he was always eager for a chance to make these little trips because they afforded a rare opportunity to play with boys at the neighbor's house.

Of course, the following Saturday, it might be the neighbor's turn to butcher and to send fresh meat to Joe's family.

No part of today's school curriculum does as much for a boy's mind as did these sorts of trips for your grandfather when he was a little boy. He had time to think. He had to be courageous. And he had to do things on his own.

Operation Hold-Off

Many of our great capitalists, bankers, and professional men, who today are sitting in air-conditioned comfort, will recognize this picture as representing one of the most hazardous of jobs.

The homesteader did not have any special breed of dairy cattle. He simply drove a few likely-looking prairie cows into the cow pen. Milking these cows for the first time was no simple task. The cow had to be roped and tied to the fence, then her hind legs tied with a "leg string" (hundreds of boys have been whipped with this!) while the homesteader milked diligently, to get a pint or so of milk.

The cow, of course, eventually became gentle, and did not have to be tied, and the task of milking became rather simple for the father. But for the boy, matters grew worse.

The calf, which it was his job to "hold off" while his dad milked, grew bigger. The calf usually "sat back" on the rope, which, if slacked would permit the calf to turn around and drag the boy through the cow pen slush and, in the process, upset the father, and the boy would get a licking.

On the other hand, if the boy was rough and held the rope too tightly, the calf would choke down and fall out for awhile, and the lad was likely to get a second licking.

Finally the milking would be over and the calf allowed to return to its mother, and the boy and his father would go into the house for supper. Then came the third possibility of trouble. The boy was supposed to go out after supper to separate the cow and calf so that there would be milk in the morning. Sometimes the lad forgot to do this, and the oversight became, when there was no milk for the family breakfast, the possibility of a third licking.

The writer, after having served in two world wars, is willing to guarantee that this was the most hazardous of assignments.

51

Spending Money

REMEMBER that this little book is a story of how people got along before the days of Government help. Here we have a trapper in the Gulf Coast marshes. This is a winter season avocation of the homesteader, by which he hopes to get enough hides from minks, otters, muskrats, and coons, to buy clothes and other "store bought" items for his wife and children, whom he has left behind on the homestead.

He perhaps reached the trapping grounds by a little sail boat or even by a pulling skiff, because there were no outboard motors then!

Trapping was not only very hard but very lonely work.

Running the "Trap Line"

This picture shows the trapper making the rounds of his muskrat traps in a saltwater marsh. The mounds which you see are muskrat hills.

On his back he is carrying a sack of muskrats, and in his left hand a stick which he uses in killing the rats before he takes them out of the trap.

Carrying this sack over two or three miles of trap line was perhaps one of the hardest jobs which the homesteader undertook.

More Spending Money

In the bayous of the Gulf Coast country, hunting alligators for hides provided many homesteaders with extra money.

Here we have a man pulling a skiff down the stream while his companion sits in the front of the boat with a shotgun or rifle and a firepan on his shoulder. It is night time. If and when he sees two fiery glows on the surface of the water, he fires his gun, with mixed success, for the alligator is a tough reptile, and making the first shot fatal is difficult.

Marsh Hunting

This is alligator hunting of a different kind. It is day time. The two men are wading the marshes with a long pole having a hook on the end. The alligator holes for which they are looking are indicated by a luxurious growth of high green marsh grass. The hunter probes the hole with his pole and hopes to succeed in hooking the alligator and in pulling him to the surface, when he kills him with a hatchet or hammer.

There are tales that this was not so simple a task and that a very large alligator could give quite a battle to men fighting him in waistdeep water.

Duck Dinner

Hunting has always been a rather enjoyable activity for Americans. Here we have a homesteader crawling up on a flock of ducks, where he hopes to get fresh meat for his family. In many cases, he hunted for the markets. In famous New Orleans restaurants, as well as in cafes of smaller towns, wild duck was on the menu as late as 1908 or 1909.

The homesteader's horse is tied in a clump of bulrushes in the background.

57

Banking Sweet Potatoes for the Winter

Both sweet and Irish potatoes were common staple food of the Gulf Coast people in homesteading days. The Irish potatoes were usually spread out on the ground under the house or in a barn where by being kept cool and dry they could be prevented from rotting for several weeks.

Sweet potatoes, however, were banked for the winter. The potatoes were dug out of the ground, hauled out of the field on a slide or wagon, or in buckets, as the boy is doing in this picture. Straw or corn stalks were first put on the ground; the potatoes were piled on top, and then covered with hay or straw, as the negro is doing in the picture, and last, dirt was thrown over the pile and the potatoes "banked" as shown in the picture.

Sweet potatoes are indeed a great treat when properly baked and served with wild duck.

This is the first picture in which a negro has been represented. As a matter of fact, to be consistent, probably all the preceding pictures should have included negroes.

Some of these negroes were faithful ex-slaves who stayed with their "families" until death, even after the Emancipation Proclamation. Too much cannot be said in praise of these loyal servants.

True enough, certain customs and habits, now called "discrimination," were practiced, but it is doubted very seriously if the oldtimers, white or black, thought very much about racial prejudice or social equality. Their mode of living was taken for granted and white and black struggled together for their common existence.

Cow Peas

ONE OFTEN hears the oldtimers speak of the delicious combination of turnip greens, cornbread, and cow peas. This picture has to do with the cow peas. Perhaps every member of the family went at odd times into the corn field to pick cow peas, these having been planted among the corn at its last working, a practice which the settlers called "laying by" the corn crop.

After sacks of peas had been gathered and allowed to dry out, the pods were spread out on a sheet and allowed to dry further in the hot sun. As soon as they were dry enough, some member of the family, using a stick or twig, beat the pods until they released the peas. The dry pods were thrown away and the residue placed in a pan. Mother "winded" the peas, as illustrated in the picture, by holding the pan high and pouring the peas onto another sheet and allowing the wind to blow away the chaff. This had to be repeated several times in order to get the peas perfectly clean, at which time they were placed in a jug and sealed tightly with a corn cob stopper.

Cow peas were one of the main staple foods for winter as they were so easily saved.

IMPORTANCE OF THE CORN PATCH

In this day and time, we speed down the highways and once in a while see a farmhouse, with a nearby five- or six-acre corn patch. We perhaps wonder why anyone would spend time planting such a small field of corn, because it amounts to so little.

The next three pages show how that little five- or six-acre corn patch was used as the homesteader's base of supplies when he was making his own way on the lonely homestead. First, it served as the feed for his horses, hogs, and chickens, or, when ground into meal, for his family. Second, the shucks and cobs were put to use in the various ways pictured here.

Particular attention is called to the cob with the piece of sweet potato vine wrapped about it. We must remember that the homesteader had to have food, and sweet potatoes were usually a large portion of it. Even though dry weather might prevent his planting potato vines, he would get a small patch of potatoes started anyway, by soaking corn cobs in water until they became saturated and then wrapping the potato vines around the cobs and planting the two together. Sufficient moisture was thus supplied so that the vines took root and the homesteader was assured of at least some sweet potatoes for the winter.

Fodder Pulling

At the top of the page, the man is stripping the stalks of their fragrant leaves and using two or three leaves as a band to tie the leaves into "hanks." He then bends the stalks down below the ear of corn to prevent the birds from eating the corn. The hank is then hung on one of the bent stalks to dry.

In the middle section of the illustration, the leaves have dried for two or three hours and the homesteader has collected the hanks and put them into bundles as illustrated, where they will dry a few hours more, and at the end of the day will be carried to the barn for storage in the loft. (If there are any little boys around, it is usually their job to do the stacking in the loft, a job which was as much play as work.)

Fodder pulling was usually pleasant work, and the smell of drying fodder leaves is an agreeable one indeed.

Incidentally, cow peas can be seen entwined about the stalks of corn. These had been broadcast among the corn when the farmer "laid by" the corn. During the spring or early summer, the homesteader picked cow peas for his dinner. The ones seen here have ripened by fodder pulling time, and the pods are yellow and will probably be picked as seed for next year's sowing.

Sunday Go To Meeting

The home, the church, the school—the foundation stones of America! The history of our country consistently shows that when a few pioneers formed a community, a church was soon organized. The church was the community center, not only for religious worship but for the social life of the settlers.

The sketch on the opposite page is of a community center that actually existed. The homes in the background, although changed by certain additions, still stand. The schoolhouse behind the church has been replaced, but originally it, with the two out-houses, was there as represented.

The chinaberry trees have long since died, but others have sprung up.

People of the settlement came from all directions to the church. The means of transportation ranged from the swanky surreys down to the everyday buggies. After singing hymns and listening to a long sermon, everybody went out for dinner on the grounds. The wives exchanged cooking recipes and talked about their babies, much as mothers and wives do today. Little children, hanging to their mothers' skirts, were probably asking for a piece of cake or pie or just crying.

The central figure of the group is the local preacher who at that time held the respect of everybody.

In the foreground, three teen-age girls have gone off to themselves to talk about their boy friends, as girls have done through the ages.

After the dinner table was cleared and a short period of gossip enjoyed, everyone went back into the church about 3 o'clock for another long sermon.

Everybody had a good time, except the poor horses, which were usually tied to the fence or post all day, perhaps without food or water.

Gulf Coast Ranches

PREVIOUS paragraphs in this little book indicated the beginning of the cattle industry. The Gulf Coast was well adapted to cattle raising because it provided green grass in the salt marshes during the winter and prairie grasses on the upland prairies during the summer.

Present-day boys and girls have been wrongly educated by the motion pictures concerning the local cattle industry. The western cowboy in the mesquite country, with his chaps and chuck wagon, was an entirely different person from the marsh cowhand.

Gulf Coast cattlemen usually wore knee boots or just ordinary heavy shoes. They wore simple spurs without all the bells and trimmings seen worn by cowboys in the motion pictures. Sometimes the Gulf Coast cowhand fastened his spurs to his shoes with a leather strap buttoned with an ornamental silver 25-cent piece. Some local blacksmith usually had the reputation of being a good spur maker.

There were few Mexican cowhands in this section of the country, but many negro cowhands, just as there are today. Many of the cowhands, and the boss always, wore a simple suit vest, not so much for its protection as for the convenience of its four pockets, in which were kept a small pencil or two, a little note pad, and usually Bull Durham tobacco. And those who could afford one wore a plain Stetson hat, not the drugstore cowboy kind with its upturned edges.

Having clipped and untangled the manes from their horses, the cowboys in this illustration are, with the aid of a tarrabee, twisting the horse hair into bridle reins or hair-hope.

On the outside back wall of the barn hangs a saddle, probably made on a Harmon saddle tree, without the humps on either side of the pommel that modern saddles have.

The old cowhands, when riding a horse they knew would jump, usually rolled a slicker and tied it to the front of the saddle for protection.

The "stiffbit" bridle hanging on the barn wall may have been made by the same blacksmith who made the spurs in that particular vicinity. Notice, also, the branding hooks, branding irons, hair rope, cow whip, spurs, a rolled slicker, and a girth (pronounced "girt" by all cowhands).

To men who were brought up on one of these early combination farm-and-ranch homesteads, there were few fond recollections. The work was hard and dirty. The next time you go to a rodeo, notice how little appeal it has for the man who was actually born and reared on one of these cattle ranches.

Branding and Marking

THIS is a typical branding pen of early days. The cattle are herded up in a corner of the pasture where the boys and less experienced help work the outer fringes of the herd to keep the cattle together.

One of the owners will have ridden into the herd on a cutting horse (more later on this subject) and will have cut out the cows and their calves, with everybody trying to remember which calf belongs to which mother.

A few head of cows and calves will have been driven into the pen with the help of a chute out in front. The cattle may belong to several owners, and the cowhands have to be careful to put the same brand on the calf which is on its mother, in order to keep ownership straight.

The boy on the outside is handing the hot branding irons and hooks through the fence to the man doing the branding inside. One cowhand has roped, thrown, and is now holding down a calf about to be branded and ear marked.

You who read this story, ask some of the oldtimers what kind of work it was inside this branding pen where the cattle had been herded for several days, especially if in the meantime there had been a rain or two. (Did you ever try to run a hot branding iron over a wet calf?)

CALF ROPING

DURING the past few years, lunch rooms with such names as the Round-Up, the Rancho, etc., frequently have on their tables menu cards showing cowboys roping steers. Calendars hanging on the walls of offices often have the same subject. Most of these pictures must be offensive to real stockmen, since they generally show the cowhand holding a rope incorrectly or throwing the rope from impossible positions.

The above paragraph is the only excuse for this additional picture, which is my feeble effort to represent how the real cowhand usually handles his rope. In the first place, the Gulf Coast cowhand, of the homesteading period, especially, did most of his roping in a branding pen. Generally he was roping calves. No cowhand, in the old days, would get into a branding pen wildly swinging his rope over his head and yelling, "Ki-yi-yippy-yippy-ay!" He would have been chased off by the boss immediately.

The above picture shows an experienced cowhand quietly preparing to throw his rope over a calf's head. He is as quiet

Shifts to back
if he has time —

J.V.

as he can be because he does not want the cattle disturbed, and
he wants to be sure which calf belongs to which mother, since
the same brand goes on both. Boisterousness in a branding pen
is the last thing the boss wants. He usually says, "Boys, let
them settle down so the calves will get with their mothers."

To watch an experienced roper in his graceful achievement is
as pleasing as watching a ballet dancer or a tennis or golf player.
He takes his coiled rope in his left hand, holding the end with
his little finger and the coils of the rope between the other
three fingers and his thumb. With his right hand he flips about
a four-foot noose to the rear and in the same motion slides his
hand about twenty inches from the rope ring. The trigger finger
of the right hand is also the trigger finger of the roper. Without swinging the rope above his head, he gently steps forward
with his weight on the left foot and then, using a follow-through
as in a golf drive or tennis serve, and bringing his right foot
forward, he throws the noose over the calf's head. If the throw
is successful, he immediately braces himself by his right foot as

shown in the picture above and, in the same instant, flips his left hand around to the small of his back to use his body as a fulcrum. If he has time, he passes the rope around his body and uses his back waist as the fulcrum, as indicated in the lower picture.

If the calf is small, he will approach it in a hand-over-hand procedure down the rope. He proceeds to "flank" the calf by throwing him to the ground and placing his right knee in the flank he has just released. The right knee is also used as illustrated.

(There have been absurd pictures of branding which represent a man holding the calf down on the belly side. Any old stockhand knows this is the business end of the calf and he would have his pants kicked off in such a position. Perhaps in the West, on the open range, they may use a different method, but this is the Gulf Coast country method.)

Flanking the Calf

On the following page is a drawing illustrating how a calf is flanked. This consists of reaching over the calf's back while holding him with the left hand by the noose around his neck, and, with a simultaneous pull with the right hand and nudge with the right knee, flopping the calf's belly out so that he falls to the ground.

In the upper picture, the calf has fallen, and you will notice that the cowhand has put his right knee in its flank. Reaching between the calf's hind legs for its tail, the cowhand uses this as a sort of rope to hold the calf in such a position as to prevent his getting traction.

At this point, the cowboy doing the branding approaches the calf from the same position which you have while reading this. The calf is branded on its right rump. When and if the calf grows up to be an old range cow like the one pictured here and is sold to another ranch she is counterbranded on the ribs, and if she is sold again, she is again counterbranded on the shoulder, the brand farthest forward being that of the latest owner.

With today's better bred cattle, there is much less branding, and probably very little ear-marking, since the stockmen do not care to disfigure their fine stock. However, the old marsh cattle were not only branded as calves but ear-marked as illustrated at the top of the page. A peculiar jargon of the old stockmen described these ear-marks. For example, the cow at the left has a "crop and saw-set" in her right ear and a "swallow fork and under-figure-7" in her left ear. The cow in the center has a "crop and hole" in her right ear and a "staple" in her left ear. The cow on the right has an "upper slope" in her right ear and a "double saw-set" in her left ear.

The writer realizes that the language used above is probably peculiar to one section and that there may have been dozens of other ways of describing these same marks.

The margins are made from recorded brands in Chambers,

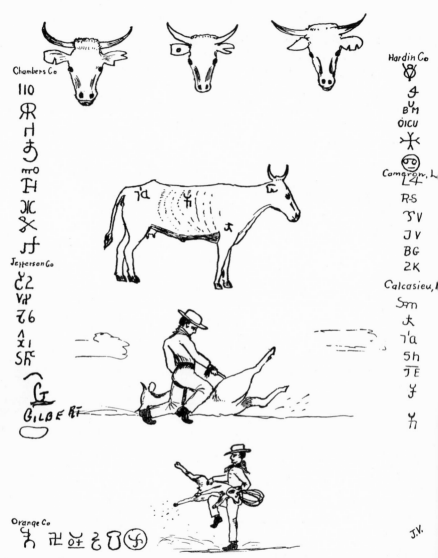

Chambers Co

110

Hardin Co

Cameron, L.

Jefferson Co

Calcasieu,

GILBERT

Orange Co

J.V.

Jefferson, Orange, and Hardin counties of Texas, and Calcasieu and Cameron parishes in Louisiana. How many can you old-timers identify?

THE ARISTOCRAT

THE ARISTOCRAT of the prairie horses was the cutting horse. These speedy little animals could "turn on a dime." As soon as they found out which cow and calf the rider wished to cut out of the herd, all the rider had to do was to manage somehow to stay on!

However, these cutting horses in most herds received their rewards because they were not ridden to ordinary tasks of herding or on long jaunts. They were specialists and were used only for "cutting."

They were usually gentle enough to permit the herd owner to walk up to them in the prairie and switch saddles from the old plug which the owner had been riding. (Of course, a handful of sugar or an ear of corn taken from the saddle bags often had a lot to do with this.)

Many are the wild tales which have been told concerning the cutting horse, some perhaps exaggerated, but he was nevertheless a great little animal and contributed no small part to the present cattle empire of the Coast.

Floating Chuck Wagon

We have said previously that the cattle industry of the Gulf Coast was a different type of operation from the dry West. It was about a three to five day trip, during the months of September or October, to drive the cattle from the summer range to the salt marshes along the Gulf Coast for winter.

These tough cowhands slushed by day through knee-deep mud and slept by night in the marsh with its myriads of mosquitoes.

At previously appointed places along the lake or river banks, a small sailing boat met the herd. This was the coastal country chuck wagon. This little sail boat was usually manned with one or two men who were both sailors and cooks for the cowhands. It was not always possible to contact the boat each night, but generally the little schooner served well. Sometimes some of the men slept on board the little vessel.

After the herd reached the marsh lands, saddles and cowhands were loaded onto the schooner where, on the trip back home, which usually required two or three days, everybody had a good time telling yarns, fishing, or duck hunting.

CROSSING STREAMS

THIS IS a close-up sketch of the schooner chuck wagon. In the foreground, cowhands are crossing a stream with their horses. Usually these horses were accustomed to the water and mud and could swim very well. The rider first tied the stirrups of the saddle to the pommel and, as the horse went into the water, slid off behind, holding to the horse's tail as it swam across the stream.

The writer does not wish to get into a big argument, but here goes! Once in a while there would be a horse that had little swimming ability. Such a horse could cross a stream only by holding his head up and being pulled across as shown here.

The writer has been told by some of the old-timers that a rider could sit upright in the saddle while his horse swam the stream. The writer does not wish to say that this is not true, but he will say that he has never seen it done. True enough, a cowhand has sat up in his saddle when he thought the horse was swimming, though actually the animal was walking across the stream on his hind feet.

You boys argue this out.

The Beef-Buyer

THIS IS the beef-buyer.

When the cattle came out of the marshes in the spring, then the beef-buyer came around. Beef was not sold by the pound then because there were no scales nearby.

Beef-buying was usually done in this way. The beef-buyer and the herd owner rode around the herd for a while, and then rode off together, and the dealing started something like this—

Beef-buyer: Mr. Smith, I will give give you $15 apiece to let me cut out 15 head of your cattle.

The Owner: Nope. I want $17 apiece.

The bargaining thus was started and ended with a compromise of, say, $16 a head.

After this trade was agreed upon, the beef-buyer, who usually rode a very fine horse, cut out his choice 15 head. Then he approached the herd owner again, with a proposal to give him $12 to let him cut out 10 head more. And so on, for most of the day, while the little boys and negro help grew very tired holding the herd together.

WINTER RANGE

A PREVIOUS picture has shown a herd of cattle being driven to the Gulf where the salt marshes were covered with green grass during the winter months. Most of the Gulf Coast has a ridge running parallel to the Gulf between the sea and the marshes. Along the ridge there was always driftwood. Hence, as wood was close at hand, houses along the Gulf usually had fireplaces.

Near the coast, trees all lean toward the north because of the prevailing south winds.

Once in a while, Gulf storms drive the tide over the beach and across the ridge, drowning many cattle in the marshes.*

In the background of this picture is the smoke from a marsh fire which has been started by the cattlemen to "burn the range." This was usually done in August so that fresh green grass would cover the scarred marshlands when the cattle were driven in during September or October.

Some of the houses on the Gulf Coast have the look-out on top, as pictured here. This is used for two purposes: to keep an eye on the whereabouts of the cattle out in the marshes, and, in the old days, to look out over the Gulf for the small schooners which plied the coast line. Some of these schooners carried lumber to such ports as Galveston and Brownsville, from the sawmilling country around the Trinity, Sabine, and Calcasieu Rivers. On the return trips, these little ships usually brought "store-bought" goods, such as furniture, cooking utensils, or clothing materials.

In Salem, Massachusetts, the counterpart of the look-out on these coastline houses is called the "widow's walk," where the wives and sweethearts watched and waited for their men folks on the fishing boats.

---

*More than 500 people lost their lives here during Hurricane Audrey in 1959.

85

PROVIDENCE RICE

THE PRAIRIE country north of the saltwater marshes of the Gulf Coast is now a vast rice domain, and this section exports probably more rice than any other section of the United States. Rice-growing is a big business in Southeast Texas and Southwest Louisiana. The great rice farms of this section had a very humble beginning.

Before the Twentieth Century, rice-growing began as "Providence patches" of the homesteaders, an expression which carried the implication that needed rain for the growth of the rice crop would come only as a gift of God. It was not a money crop, in the beginning, but simply an item to supplement the garden produce and to provide a winter food which could be easily stored. If the season was wet, there would be a good stand; if it was dry, there would be no rice.

Here we have the homesteader sowing rice by hand in a small seed bed which he has prepared in a "flat" or low place where water will collect when there is rain. Perhaps he did this with a prayer for rain on his lips.

Rice Harvest

EVIDENTLY these homesteaders have been blessed by rain during the summer months because here they are harvesting what looks like a heavy crop of rice.

The man is using a cradle (not a scythe) for cutting the rice. Each time he swings the cradle, he slides the rice stalks off the fingers of the cradle in neat piles. Sometimes it was his wife who came behind, gathering up the bunches and tying them together in bundles which she arranged in a shock, as shown. When a half dozen or so bundles were stacked together with their heads up, a cap was formed by slipping the band holding the bundles together toward the rice heads and inverting the bundles, pulling the buts of the straw out in such a way as to form a roof for the shock, which prevented the rice birds from eating the grain.

This method of harvesting rice was followed years later by first the binders and then the combines, with which we are now familiar.

Early Threshing

After the rice had remained in shock long enough to dry, it was ready for threshing. Before the days of the mechanical rice thresher, the homesteader removed the grain from the straw as shown here. It was a simple but arduous process. Taking a handful of straw at a time, he whipped the grain off into a barrel. Sometimes he saved the straw to be used as hay for the cow during the winter. Sometimes he left the straw on the ground for the chickens to finish threshing.

Here, the homesteader has sought a cool place in the shade of a friendly chinaberry tree in the rear of his house. When he has finished beating the rice off the straw, he will pour it into sacks and perhaps store it under the bed in his home.

One of the advantages of rice as a staple food was that it could easily be saved for winter use. Rice with wild duck gravy is perhaps the most palatable of all foods (writer's opinion).

The back porch of this home is typical of those of the day. Hanging on the wall of the house are the drinking gourd and the drying onions, pepper, and garlic in plaited strings. On the wash shelf are an old red cedar bucket, the wash pan, and soap box. Hanging from the line are the family towel and a sack of clabbered milk, which, when all the whey has drained out, will be good old cream or cottage cheese.

POUNDING RICE

THIS looks like the same home as the one on the previous page, but some time later. The woman of the house is here cleaning rice by using a mortar and pestle.

The mortar was made by chipping little holes in the end of a four-foot cut of log, building a fire in the holes and, by alternate burning and chipping, smoothing a recess in the wood block.

The pestle was a piece of hardwood, finished to suit the desire of the maker.

You will notice that this woman has been at other hard work: the family washing. The wash pot, the wooden tub, and rub-board are nearby. Perhaps her husband has made the tub by sawing the end off a whiskey or lard barrel, which he has "spoken for" previously at the store where he buys his coffee and sugar and hardware.

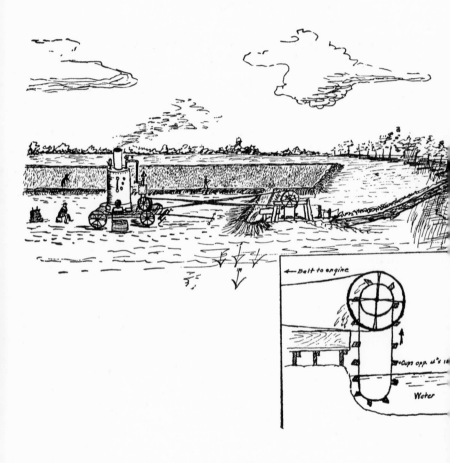

← Belt to engine

+Cups opp. 16's 16

Water

94

FLOODING RICE

JUST when the first rice patch was artificially irrigated in the Gulf Coast is, to the writer, not a matter of records. It can be stated, however, and supported by record, that in 1879, William Vincent irrigated approximately twenty acres of rice near Choupique Bayou, approximately twenty miles northwest of what is now Hackberry, Louisiana.

The little 8-horsepower engine sketched here, and which ran the pump, was sold for old iron about the year 1915. The simple little boiler was fired with wood, the water being provided from the barrel, as illustrated in the sketch. The water was forced into the boiler by a pump; there was no injector.

The engine was of so much interest to the writer that he believes he remembers practically every detail of it and that this sketch is fairly accurate.

The pump illustrated here was burned as old trash about 1908. The drawing is simply an estimation of how the pumping plant must have looked, judging by traces of the old ditch and levees which were still perceptible as late as 1916.

Levees were made by first throwing them up as high as possible with a large plow pulled by oxen. They were then further worked into shape by a homemade "levee push." Final touches were put to the levees by a man with a shovel.

If any oldtimer reading this little book knows of an earlier rice irrigation project, information concerning it will be appreciated by the writer.

The Yankees Came

As a little boy in 1903 to 1905, I remember my old rebel great-grand-dad fuming because the Yankees were sweeping the country. News had spread north about the rice boom. Irrigation canals were built by these energetic and thrifty people who came from the Middle West wheat fields and brought with them fine mules, binders, and other improved methods.

The newcomers further amazed the earlier settlers by building larger and better barns than homes. They built what were to the Southern homesteaders funny houses with one room above the other. But it soon became apparent that such constructoin was thrifty because the homesteader was able to have more rooms under the same roof.

Many of these new citizens became leaders in their communities. They turned out to be pretty good folks. As a matter of fact, I married one of them.

LUMBER

SEVENTY-FIVE years ago, the many streams which fed the Gulf
of Mexico wound their serpentine ways through vast forests of
pine, hardwood, and cypress trees. Over a hundred years ago,
people began settling on the banks of these bayous and rivers.
They fashioned their homes of logs and boards cut and hewn
from the forests. It was quite natural that the lumber industry
should spring up along the banks of many of these streams because of the water transportation to the outside world. Towns
such as Beaumont and Orange, Texas, and Lake Charles, Louisiana,
had as their beginning a river wharf, a country store, and a small
sawmill. Examination of the old store ledgers reveals that the
country store was a sort of trading post. Usually one man
owned the sawmill, the store, and wharf, and sometimes he had
one or more coastwise schooners.

In the beginning, logs were simply cut from the Government-
owned land, sawed into lumber, and sold for $2 or $3 a thousand,
provided the lumber dealer got the job of transporting the
lumber in his schooner to Galveston and other coastal towns,
for which service he charged $26 a thousand feet.

The flat-bottomed boat with the windlass in the foreground
was used to raise cypress logs which had sunk to the bottom
of the river.

Settlements of this sort were finally known as "landings."
Down the Calcasieu River from Lake Charles, for example, in
order, were Pujo's Landing, Broussard's Landing, Lyons Landing
(the owners of the latter two landings were the maternal and
paternal grandfathers of Dr. S. B. Lyons of Beaumont, Texas),
West's Landing (owned by the grandfather of Mrs. Lyons),
Vincent's Landing, Haymark Landing, Johnson's Landing, Drost

Landing, and finally, Cameron, Louisiana, at the mouth of the river. Every one of these landings had its sawmill and store, and if there had been chambers of commerce in those days, their mottoes would probably have been, "Where the ox teams of the area meet the schooners of the sea."

Oldtimers have stated that before the Southern Pacific Railroad came through the area, at any one of these landings could be seen sails of from twenty-five to thirty schooners. The landings were busy places, where people came from miles around by ox teams to trade their logs and cow hides for shoes, calico, coffee, and sometimes whiskey.

A Landing

THIS is a sailor's view from the deck of a little schooner coming up the river. In the distance, we see ox teams coming to the store; three sailboats, a lugger, a sloop, and a two-masted schooner are lying at anchor, waiting to discharge or receive cargo. The boats are probably engaged in river trade, since they are small. More about this later.

It may be added that these stores more or less functioned as a social club for the men. Wagons brought settlers and ships brought sailors who loafed in the stores telling yarns and at times imbibing too freely of the whiskey which was sold without license (not required at the time).

Sailor Settlers

When the sea-going schooners came up the rivers and bayous of the Gulf Coast, true to world history, some of the sailors found girls in the ports, married them, and became local citizens. Tiring of the sea and unfamiliar with the ways of making a living in the new country, the sailors naturally reached to the jobs they knew: boats. So they built little flat-bottomed schooners and sloops, such as these, and worked the river trade, boating lumber to new sites on the rivers and up its tributaries, or, if they were fishermen, bringing oysters from the saltwater oysterbeds.

These river-plying ships usually had such names as Edith, Emma, Clara, Mary, etc. Sometimes the wives and families lived on the boats. At Moss Lake, which is a part of the Calcasieu River, is a settlement which used to be called Dutch Cove, a community which was settled mostly by people who came in on schooners and established themselves there, becoming prominent citizens in the State. Such names as Hansen, Olsen, Jensen, Halverson, Drost, and Thompson, indicate the background and nature of these fine people. Many of their descendants are now merchants and professional men of that section of Louisiana, serving on civic and school boards.

THE LUGGERS

ABOUT the turn of the century, newspaper headlines announced the kidnapping of a child in New Orleans by the Black Hand Society. Such a story at that time created considerable commotion in the small communities. Most of the luggers (the boat here pictured) were manned by Italian fishermen who sold oysters and fish to the various landings along the river. Since the Black Hand Society was known as an Italian society, naturally the children on the river banks became afraid of the luggers, especially those with red sails.

The main break in the routine of life for children who lived along the rivers and bayous was watching the boats pass. After the story of the kidnapping spread, boys and girls retreated to the nearby woods whenever they saw the sails of the luggers.

This story is told to indicate how important the luggers became in the lives of children who lived along the meanders of the rivers and bayous of the section.

In the skiff in the foreground is a man spending his leisure time as did most of the river bank folks.

Transportation Schooners

THE writer's frequent references to the Calcasieu are not meant to glorify any particular river or section of Southwest Louisiana and Southeast Texas, but it is believed that the Calcasieu River, the only river with which the writer is thoroughly familiar, was typical of the other rivers which penetrated the Gulf Coast lowlands, such as the Trinity, Brazos, Neches, and Sabine in Texas, and the Mermentau River and the Bayou Teche in Louisiana.

This is a memory drawing of a "scow schooner," a boat which actually transported thousands of feet of lumber down the Calcasieu to Gulf ports such as Galveston, Harrisburg, and Point Isabel. She was named the A. J. Perkins, after an important lumberman of Lake Charles, Louisiana. Her "bones" can now be seen on the west side of Moss Lake, which is below Lake Charles.

Sail Symphony

Perhaps no sight is more beautiful than a well-modeled ship under sail. The old schooner builders were evidently master craftsmen. The Schooner A. J. Perkins, on the previous page, was simply a large scow or barge, and it was built for the purpose of transporting cargo only.

However, boats of the type pictured here, with full sails, and either with fair wind or listing to the leeward as they tacked against head winds up and down the river, were beautiful sights which will linger in the minds of the river bank children as long as life shall last.

There were many of these schooners, but especially beautiful were the George Lock (owned by another lumberman of Lake Charles), the Lehman, the C. H. Moore, and the Paul Simpson. Children used to "play like" they owned these ships, and they could recognize their own vessel by her sails as she appeared over the marsh grasses miles away.

These graceful boats supplied most of the romance, air castles, and dreams of the children who dwelt along the river banks, before the railroad came and spelled the doom of water transportation by small vessels.

THE GASOLINE-MOTORED *Olga*

THE *Olga* actually existed. She was by far the largest schooner which the boys and girls of the central Gulf Coast section had ever seen, and too, she was different, and in a way the *Olga* was the beginning of a new era in river transportation.

In about 1902 or 1903, the *Olga* was putting up the Calcasieu River with a fair wind when she struck a reach in the river where she had a head wind. She was too large to tack, and so the first gasoline motor ever heard in those parts started. The people on the river banks were amazed: here was something different, a boat with sails being pushed against the wind by some kind of engine inside which did not require a smoke stack to belch forth black smoke from a pine knot fire!

Steamboat Mail

The United States mail had been carried by sailboats up and down the river during the carpetbagger days, following the Civil War, but regular and dependable routine for the transpotration of mail up and down the rivers came with the steamboat. The little stern-wheeled Harvey here pictured was carrying the mail to Cameron, Louisiana, during the latter period of the Gay 90's. She would leave Lake Charles on Mondays for Cameron. On Tuesdays, she left Cameron for Lake Charles. On alternating days, mail was received.

One could wave a handkerchief or flag from any one of the various landings, and the Harvey would come in, take the passenger on board and for $1.50 make the trip from Lake Charles to Cameron, or vice versa. The Harvey also carried important or "fast" freight to the different landings. She was the "express" boat, while the river schooners were comparable to the slower freight trains of today.

River Steamer News Flash

THE world moves on! From the beginning of history, speed has brought change. The old Harvey was succeeded by a more beautiful lady with more graceful lines and greater speed, a steamer called the Romeo, from Saginaw, Michigan. Although it was half a century ago, the gold letters on the stern of the Romeo are still vivid to those who saw her come up the Calcasieu River on that Sunday afternoon at about the beginning of the new Century. Captain Andrews of the Romeo, smoking his cob pipe, was the hero and guardian of the river folks, as the steamer took over the mail contract. Captain Andrews was a likeable old fellow, and made it his business to see that important events were reported at strategic landings up and down the River.

On the Wednesday that was September 11, 1901, we heard one blast of the Romeo's whistle, which meant she was not going to land but to come in near the wharf to throw off a newspaper. (She would have blown three blasts if she had been going to land.) As the Romeo slowed down and came in near the landing, Captain Andrews hurled a stick to shore. Wrapped around the stick was a copy of the Lake Charles American Press with the headline, "President McKinley Shot." The attempted assassination had been five days earlier, on September 6. The people of the river bank had to wait more than a week for the trip of the Romeo which brought the sad news that President McKinley had not survived the murderous attack but had succumbed on the 14th of September.

Every Dog Has His Day

In about 1910, Captain Bowie McCain brought to the Calcasieu River a new mail boat, called the Borealis Rex. She was faster and larger, though not so beautiful, as the Romeo. However, she got the mail contract and became an institution of great importance for a decade. Captain Ben Moss was at one time the skipper of this steamer.

On Sundays, the Borealis Rex carried excursions down the River to Spanish Point, or Grand Lake. On these excursion trips, there were music and dancing, and many present-day grandmothers and grandfathers enjoyed their best courting on the decks of the Borealis Rex.

T. V. McCoy, of Beaumont, one of the leading Masons of the State of Texas, and his wife were one couple of the many whose courtship ripened aboard this steamer.

The gay young blade of Lake Charles who had not taken his girl on an excursion on the Borealis Rex had simply just not arrived!

Road Building

A COLLECTIVE struggle for existence has through the ages been the practice of most communities, tribes, and families which survive. On their own initiative, the first two or three homesteaders voluntarily got together, blazing trails through the woods or marking roads over the prairies. As the communities grew and became a part of a county or parish organization, roads were built by the people who used them.

The sheriff of the parish or county would summon the people of a community to work on the roads. Each family head had to work a certain number of days on the "public roads," or could pay an assessment, which was used to hire someone else. The appointment as boss of the road gang was quite a political plum because he earned $3 per day.

Here we have a road crew composed of people of the community who have come in wagons or on horseback to work. The horses have been staked out and one of the crew is cooking dinner or making coffee on a fire nearby.

To most of the men, building these roads and bridges was a sort of picnic, and no one worked too hard, and many yarns were told.

However, a few people resented working on the roads and even complained when they had to pay their assessment. When these assessments became taxes, our great highways had their beginning.

THE TUGBOATS

IN THE course of time, the little sawmills up and down the rivers at the landings became obsolete as the major lumber companies built large mills in Beaumont, Orange, and Lake Charles. Lumber became the leading industry, and mills built tough, sturdy tugboats for towing booms of logs up and down the rivers to the big mills. Around these sawmills grew the present towns of Beaumont, Orange, and Houston, Texas, and Lake Charles, Louisiana.

The writer happens to remember the names of four of these little tugs which plied the Calcasieu. They were the Molineaux, the Ernest, the Vivian, and the Ontario, the last having as its skipper Captain Dobertine.

The Little School House

JUST as the neighbors got together to build roads, they also joined in building other community projects, such as the school house. These structures ranged all the way from a palmetto arbor-shade to a fairly nice little one-room building. They were well or badly constructed, depending upon the ability and skill of the local "carpenter." (Let us keep in mind that every community had its self-appointed specialists. One man, for instance, would have a reputation for knowing something about machinery, another carpentering, and the Justice of the Peace, if any, was consulted in matters of the law.)

Here is sketched an average one-room school, erected by the united efforts of the homesteaders who probably paid for most of the lumber, with an allowance of perhaps two or three hundred dollars from the county or parish seat. It is well constructed, but like practically all one-room schools of the day, it was poorly lighted and built along the lines of the settlers' homes, without regard for the purpose it was to serve.

The teacher is sweeping out the sand carried in onto the floor during the morning by bare feet. She probably does not have a State certificate but has a reputation for being a "smart woman" in the community. Or perhaps she has a high school diploma. This would have been rather high standing for the teachers of the day. Her salary, perhaps $30 per month, was paid by patrons who "chipped in" to make up the amount, and she probably "boards around" among the community's settlers.

Eleven children are in sight. Two little girls are at the front door of the building, admiring their teacher, or, perhaps, just "polishing their apple."

The two boys in the background have gone to a neighboring house for a bucket of drinking water which they have suspended between them on a stick and are carrying to the school house where the bucket will perhaps be placed on a box in the corner, with the common drinking cup, which may have been fashioned out of a dried gourd and hangs on the wall above.

The three boys and the girl near the building are playing "one-o-cat," which was the standard game of the rural schools where not enough children were present to organize a regular baseball game. The little boys reluctantly included the girls in these games, in order to have enough to play. The game was played with only a home-run plate and a first base. When the batter hit the ball, he ran to first base and back, whereupon he became pitcher, the next player, catcher, and the next, the first baseman. Every fellow kept his own score, and the game was played for individual honors and not for team honors, because there were no teams.

The three boys in the foreground have finished eating their lunch, brought to school in lard buckets. Their lunch was probably composed of a baked sweet potato, a couple of biscuits and a couple of hard-boiled eggs, all of which, of course, were cold. Having finished their lunch, they are playing a game which is not now popularly known, called "500." In this game, someone produced a pocket knife and fully opened the small blade and half opened the large blade. The players took turn about flipping the knife up into the air from the resting position here shown. If the knife stuck up on the smaller blade, the player earned 50 points, on the larger, 20 points, if it lay on its back, 40 points, and if it fell on its side, he scored nothing, and the next boy took the knife for his try. When one of the players reached a total of 500, the game was over, except that the boy with the lowest score had to pull a peg from the ground with his teeth which the winner had driven into the ground as far as he could in three blows, using the knife for a hammer.

Mumble-peg produced much enthusiasm, and, sometimes, fights. In some circles the game was frowned upon by parents because the knife had been known to stick into the leg of a player.

Perhaps when the next noon hour comes around, all the school will join in a game of pop-the-whip, or chip-pile.

Much could be said about the crude furnishing of the school with its hard benches, home-made desks, and so forth, but it would be no different from what has been said many times before of all one-room country schools.

THE PIONEER DENTIST

Much has been written giving information of and praise to the pioneer doctors, preachers and peddlers who followed in the wake of a rugged people as they moved in search of land into the interior of our American continent. They were more than is indicated by their specialty for they brought much desired news, homely advice, and a new social contact to the lonely settler.

Little, if anything, however, has been written about the early dentists. Homesteaders usually simply endured toothache, which they treated with home remedies such as hot salt packs or toothache bark from the thorny toothache tree (*Aralia Spinosa*), until the family doctor, who always carried forceps, came and pulled the offensive tooth.

In the latter part of the nineteenth century traveling dentists made their appearance in the lowlands of Southwest Louisiana and Southeast Texas. One of these, who referred to his professional circuit riding as "working" a community, was Dr. Van Brook. Traveling in a little covered wagon drawn by a single bay horse, he would, if any dental work were needed, stay for

126

several days at a settler's home, where he and his horse were both fed. In the mornings he worked on the plates of patients of homes previously visited and in the afternoons treated the members of the family where he was staying. If a set of teeth had to be made, he delivered them on his return.

The memory drawing shows Dr. Van Brook's little prairie schooner. Its dentist's chair, foot-operated drill, chest of bright, shiny dental instruments, and bedding roll and food, in case he had to camp overnight on the road, constituted a thrill to little boys who had never seen any but rather seedy work horses, simple farm tools, and plain work clothes.

The wagon shafts are shown leaning on one of two oaklings which are now widespreading trees, with Spanish moss hanging from them onto the roof of a home, which today is the center of a prosperous rice farm and cattle ranch, only a few miles over concrete roads from modern clinics.

The Best School I Ever Attended

After we had "proven up" the homestead, (five years) we had grown prosperous. We sold one hundred and twenty dollars' worth of wool. Among other things, Papa bought Mama a new Majestic range and a pair of high-top, button Julia Marlowe shoes. The stove had the figure of a ship on the oven door. Of course it required the same old wood box which held the wood consumed by its predecessor, the old black iron four-hole Garland stove which we sold for $3. These new "store bought" things brought us much happiness and pride, because it was apparent to us that we were going to "make it".

"We should all be happy because, although we may have a hard time on earth, we will go to that place of everlasting happiness: Heaven. And it is so easy," she said, "because God gave us a few simple rules to go by, the Ten Commandments and the two great commandments. Now, of course, there is another place for bad people who disobey God's rules. There they are in torment forever and ever. But this is a good family and we need not worry." It was that simple!

Once a month when the *Ladies' Home Journal* came, Mama read to us, "Two Little Savages" and "Wild Animals I Have Known" which Ernest Thompson Seton wrote for the magazine. Of course there were also stories about the gallantry of Admiral Dewey, Roosevelt at San Juan and the sinking of the *Maine* in the recent Spanish-American War. She also told us stories of Washington and Lee and other great Americans. She was a great teacher and a great adopted American, who once in a while reminded us, with a sweet twinkle in her eyes, that "the sun never sets on the British Empire."

Over half a century has passed, and I now know that the most important thing to us was that old wood box, because we kids used to sit in it and listen to Mama, who was a gentle and sweet Canadian-born woman, "tell us things."

The End of the Beginning

There had been various tales in the central Gulf Coast section that hinted of the coming of oil. Some of the tales told by the old settlers mentioned the old lake where the ox carts driven from the big woods to the landings would stop to grease their thimbles with the substance floating on top of the pond. Years later, this became the site of the Union Sulphur Company.

There was the tale that at Hackberry, Louisiana, where it was hard to get fresh water in the summer, somebody drilled a well for water and had been able to light the peculiar sort of gas which escaped from the hole.

These and other rumors became fact when, on January 10, 1901, Captain Anthony Lucas brought in the Spindletop gusher at Beaumont, Texas. This was "the beginning of a new era in civilization." Other fields were discovered, such as the Sour Lake, Saratoga, Batson, Jennings, and Sulphur fields.

Nothing so changed the pattern of living in the Gulf Coast country as the discovery of oil. The orderly, peaceful routine of the homesteaders' lives was disturbed beyond belief. Men who otherwise would have been farmers or ranchers flocked to the oil fields. Those who remained on the farmlands became truck farmers with a voracious market in the neighboring oil fields.

After a few years, gasoline made possible the farm tractors, the automobile, and the truck, all of which were important factors in ushering in the new age. Hence the ending of this story.

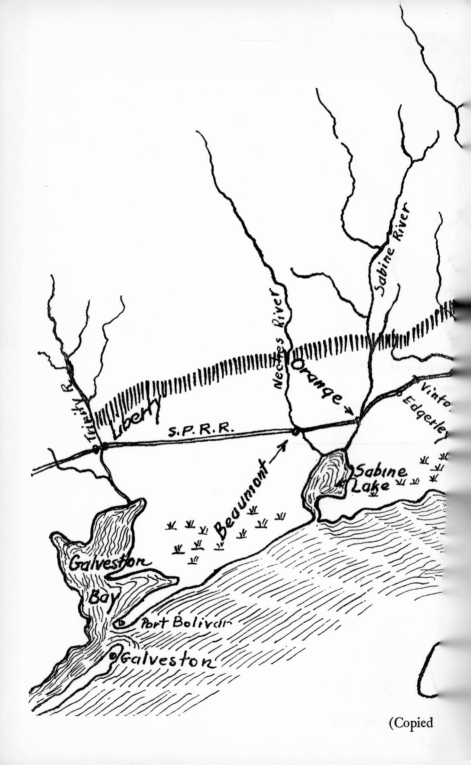

(Copied